D1328425

41 Blessings
Reflection Journal

Creating
A New U!

41 Blessings Reflection Journal

Creating A New U!

RICHONDA HILL

Editorial Midwife Publishing

Copyright © 2022 by Richonda Hill

Ordering Information

Quantity sales: Special discounts are available on quantity purchases by corporations, associations, and others. Orders by trade bookstores and wholesalers: Contact Richonda at anewu18@gmail.com for more information.

Editor & Consultant

LPW Editing & Consulting Services, LLC
Editorial Midwife Publishing
lpwediting@gmail.com

ISBN: 9798439271887

Table of Contents

41 Blessings
Reflection Journal

"Creating A New U!"

This Devotional Journal
belongs to:

Name: _____

Introduction

This 41-day blessing journal encompasses various inspiring and motivating blessings to challenge you to become the ultimate version of yourself. Each page is devoted to speaking blessings over your life and provides the extra support you need to live a fulfilled life. In addition, each page is titled per blessing, allowing you to reflect and journal, focusing on a specific journal entry.

If you are an aspiring author, allow "41 Blessings" to jump-start your very own journal or book. After writing your reflections in "41 Blessings," take each reflection that you have written and begin your journey of developing your own reflection journey.

You will find that this journal will be beneficial even after you reach Day 41. We all are constantly evolving and need constant reminders to thrive, no matter how complex a situation is. God has an excellent plan for you! So get ready to experience the joy of counting your blessings one day at a time.

~x~

Blessing 1: Encourage Yourself

David encouraged himself in the LORD his God.
(1 Samuel 30:6b)

Today, I want you to focus on encouraging yourself. I want you to say ten positive things to and about yourself. Write those things down. For example, *I am successful. I am setting goals and crushing them. I am debt-free.* Take the time to write those encouraging affirmations about yourself.

On those days that you may feel under the weather or just not as high-spirited as you usually do, reflect back on the words you spoke and wrote about yourself.

Now, take a moment and think about a situation you thought was a failure. Then, reflect on the positive outcome of that situation. Reflect on how the positive outweighed the negative. Just like that experience turned out positively, all other situations that you face will work out for your good as well.

Continue to encourage yourself. Remember that every trial comes to develop a skill that you will need along this journey called life. You've got this!

Blessing 1: Encourage Yourself

My Reflections

_____

_____

_____

_____

_____

_____

_____

_____

_____

_____

_____

_____

_____

_____

My Blessings

Blessing 2: Love You

*I will praise thee; for I am fearfully
and wonderfully made:
(Psalms 139:14a)*

Today, I want you to focus on love. Love is a special four-letter word. It is special because there is so much that is attached to it. Love can be so positive, but the attachments can seem negative. For example, we love people that sometimes don't reciprocate that same love back. Also, sometimes we lose loved ones, and the feelings from the loss of love feel negative. All in all, love is beautiful.

It's more about a person's perception. It's all about how you perceive such a thing called love. Let's remember the love that Jesus had and still has for us. The pain He endured because of His love for us. Just because love can have its highs and lows doesn't mean you have to stop loving. Love is beautiful in life. Just do your part, and the rest will follow how it's orchestrated.

Now, take a moment to reflect on an important piece to the puzzle, self-love. Remember, before you can genuinely show love, you must love yourself. You were created uniquely in your own way. Take a few minutes to write down what love means to you and those things that you love about yourself. Then, reflect on those things throughout the day. You are such an astonishing person!

Blessing 2: Love You

My Reflections

_____

_____

_____

_____

_____

_____

_____

_____

_____

_____

_____

_____

My Blessings

_____

_____

_____

_____

_____

_____

_____

_____

_____

_____

_____

_____

_____

Blessing 3: You Are What You Think!

For as he thinketh in his heart, so is he:
(Proverbs 23:7a)

Today I want you to focus on your thoughts. Did you know that you are what you think? Some may say you are what you eat. However, you really are what you think. Every move that you have ever made started off with a thought. You had to think about it first. Therefore, it is so important to keep a healthy mind.

We should walk in love and maintain the mind of Christ. Maintaining a healthy mind will allow you to make healthy decisions. What are you doing to keep your mind healthy? Are you thinking positive thoughts consistently? Are you listening to or reading positive motivational books or podcasts? What is the first thing that you do in the morning?

Keep in mind that how you start your day will depict how your day will flow and the mindset that you will have. It's the small things. It is believed that you should make yourself smile every morning to boost your immune system and reduce stress. Therefore, smiling will assist with keeping your mind healthy also. Just do what you have to do to make it an amazing day, and remember to keep your mind healthy! Write down your thoughts and critique them. Are they empowering? Think of positive things daily. You *are* such a thoughtful soul!

Blessing 3: You Are What You Think!

My Reflections

_____

_____

_____

_____

_____

_____

_____

_____

_____

_____

_____

_____

_____

My Blessings

_____

_____

_____

_____

_____

_____

_____

_____

_____

_____

_____

_____

_____

_____

Blessing 4: Become Passionate

Whatever you do, work heartily, as for the Lord and not for men. (Colossians 3:23)

When you are passionate about something, you are automatically driven to it and its success. Your passion is instilled in you, and it has been there the entire time. Many people say that there is nothing that they are passionate about. That is very interesting because we all have passion within us. It is beneficial to take a moment and sit in peace and quiet to tap into your passion. Take this time to ask yourself what you are passionate about. What drives you? What excites and enthuses you? Once you identify your passion, you can begin walking in your destiny. Jot those things down. Reflect on them daily. You are passionately you!

Blessing 4: Become Passionate

My Reflections

_____

_____

_____

_____

_____

_____

_____

_____

_____

_____

_____

_____

_____

My Blessings

_____

_____

_____

_____

_____

_____

_____

_____

_____

_____

_____

_____

_____

Blessing 5: Joy

Be joyful in hope, patient in affliction, faithful in prayer.
(Romans 12:12)

J oy is defined as a feeling of great pleasure and happiness. Although this sounds pleasant and a great state, some people lack joy. Can you believe that there are people who don't allow themselves to experience great pleasure or happiness? Instead, they allow circumstances and situations to play a role in how happy or sad they are. Joy is actually a choice. Two people can be experiencing the same obstacle, and one may be happy during that time. However, the other person may look at the obstacle as defeat and allow it to rob them of their joy.

Yes, we are all human, and we do face trying situations. However, we must learn to look at the big picture and try hard to maintain a positive outlook on every situation. It is undoubtedly easier said than done. Ask yourself, "What good is going through a situation, and then once it's over, you are in the hospital because you have ulcers from stress? This is why you must trust God that everything will be okay. Putting your trust in God will allow you to experience that peace that surpasses all understanding. Remember that your attitude determines your altitude. The joy of the Lord is your strength. (Nehemiah 8:10) Continue to be encouraged and know that you must choose joy daily. Take a moment to write down those things that bring you joy. What challenges do you need to reevaluate? What is your outlook on that situation? Are you choosing joy over sadness? You are a joyful being!

Blessing 5: Joy

My Reflections

_____

_____

_____

_____

_____

_____

_____

_____

_____

_____

_____

_____

My Blessings

Blessing 6: God is so Good!

Reflecting on the goodness of the Lord and all He has done for you will make your soul rejoice. You are blessed beyond measure. The more you rest in His presence, you will gain revelation on how He has been developing you this entire time. His grace and mercy will carry you through.

Some people let degrees and accolades represent who they are. However, it's really about who you become during life's process. What type of person have you transformed into during any process? For example, when you experience situations that cause you to focus and be devoted for a period of time, a level of patience is being developed. Therefore, patience won't be a major issue when tackling other projects or life experiences. I often hear people say that certain situations made them stronger and better people. That is so true. Trouble doesn't always last.

On this journey, we will have to make a variation of pit stops or maybe even detours. Keep in mind the end, which is your destiny and purpose. Continue to focus on how God has blessed you along this journey, which will transform your perspective tremendously. Ask yourself, "Who have I become during this process called life?" You are blessed by God's goodness!

Blessing 6: God is so Good!

My Reflections

_____

_____

_____

_____

_____

_____

_____

_____

_____

_____

_____

_____

_____

My Blessings

_____

_____

_____

_____

_____

_____

_____

_____

_____

_____

_____

_____

_____

_____

Blessing 7: You've Got This

I can do all things through Christ
which strengtheneth me.
(Philippians 4:13)

As you prepare for the obstacle ahead of you, there is a drop of sweat that swiftly rolls down your face. You realize that your heart rate has increased rapidly. You feel faint and weak in your knees. Your mouth gets extremely dry, and you find it hard to swallow. You begin to see your hands tremble.

"OMG!" is what you are thinking to yourself. At that moment, you look up and see a sign that says. INSPIRE. This was just what you needed to begin thinking positively about the challenges you face. Sometimes what you need to be encouraged is right there in front of you. When faced with adversity, just look up, and what do you see?

You've got this! You can do this! There is nothing that you cannot do. Take a deep breath and think positively. You've got this. Step out on faith, overcome your fear and just do it. Think of the results of you overcoming your fear. Wipe the sweat and go! No matter what it is, just go. Write down those things that you will overcome and how you will overcome those challenges. You are a warrior!

Blessing 7: You've Got This!

My Reflections

_____

_____

_____

_____

_____

_____

_____

_____

_____

_____

_____

_____

My Blessings

Blessing 8: God's Grace

For by grace are ye saved through faith; and that not of yourselves: it is the gift of God: (Ephesians 2:8)

Rest in God and know that things will continue to work out for your good. God knows best, and He knows what you need when you need it. God is able to keep you from falling. He knows how to strengthen your every pain, heartache, and burden. Just know that all will be well. *Trust in the Lord with all thine heart and lean not on thine own understanding. In all your ways acknowledge him, and he will direct your path* (Proverbs 3:5-6).

God knows exactly what He is doing. Therefore, He deserves glory and praise in every situation. Trust God and His Word. Cast your cares on Him because He cares and sees what you are going through.

Take a moment and reflect on the goodness of the Lord. Write down those situations you know He is working on behind the scenes. All is well with you!

Blessing 8: God's Grace

My Reflections

_____

_____

_____

_____

_____

_____

_____

_____

_____

_____

_____

_____

My Blessings

_____

_____

_____

_____

_____

_____

_____

_____

_____

_____

_____

_____

_____

_____

_____

Blessing 9: To Thine Ownself be True

You are altogether beautiful, my darling,
beautiful in every way.
(Song of Solomon 4:7)

I t's amazing how the media has impacted and influenced people so heavily. People change their appearance based on an impression created by the media. Everyone is an individual. Imitating others is very risky. Please be careful how you allow the impressions of others to depict your perception of what your life should be like.

It is dangerous to live another person's purpose. God would have made us all alike if we were destined to imitate others' appearance. Instead, we are to imitate HIM. Decipher those attributes that are beneficial and that pour into your overall well-being. It's so disheartening to hear youth and adults say that they want to look like someone in the media. It's astonishing the compliments that we give others compared to how we compliment ourselves. Word to the wise, be the one that others want to imitate. Be unique. Embrace what you have because you don't know that cookies are stale until you bite into them.

Empower yourself and be the best version of yourself! Reflect and write those things that you love about yourself. How are you being true to yourself? What characteristics do others adore about you? You are beautiful!

Blessing 9: To Thine Ownself be True

My Reflections

_____

_____

_____

_____

_____

_____

_____

_____

_____

_____

_____

_____

_____

_____

My Blessings

_____

_____

_____

_____

_____

_____

_____

_____

_____

_____

_____

_____

_____

Blessing 10: Go Get What's Yours!

Commit to the Lord whatever you do, and he will establish your plans. (Proverbs 16:3)

There is unclaimed territory that you must obtain. You have heard a word and have been lax with going to get what's yours. When you claim it, claim it with enthusiasm! If it is in your heart to start a business, write a blog, write a book, lead the masses or even build an empire - Go Get It! Go get what's yours! Think back to when you were younger and enjoyed catching lightning bugs (fireflies). Just like that, you need to chase after what's yours. With that same respect, you must chase your dreams.

Why do you minimize and decrease when it comes to claiming what's yours? Why do you let your past marginalize your future? Stop catching lightning bugs and catch the light of your book, blog, empire, legacy

builder, and vision for your life. Now is the time to...
GO GET WHAT'S YOURS!

Take a moment and write about the territory that you are claiming. What is it that you have procrastinated about? You have what it takes!

Blessing 10: Go Get What's Yours!

My Reflections

_____

_____

_____

_____

_____

_____

_____

_____

_____

_____

_____

_____

_____

My Blessings

_____

_____

_____

_____

_____

_____

_____

_____

_____

_____

_____

_____

_____

_____

_____

_____

Blessing 11: Grief Care

Blessed are they that mourn: for they shall be comforted.
(Matthew 5:4)

This is not a very easy topic to discuss, but it is a straightforward topic to go unnoticed. Where do you start to type when you think about the absence of......? It's like a thought that never manifests into anything. You think of that person, and you can't do anything but think about that person and reflect on the memories. You can't help how you feel in those moments; however, you can help how you handle your feelings.

Taking deep breaths seems to work temporarily. However, the keyword here is *temporarily*. Then, the harshness of reality kicks back in. *Where do you go? Who do you talk to? What do you do? Where do you go? Who do you talk to? What do you do?* These are questions that are silently repeated in the mind. The heaviness of grief is somewhat unbearable. It seems that anything can cause emotional distress.

Seek God to help, and He sure does provide the peace that surpasses all understanding (Philippians 4:7). He also provides wisdom on the next steps. Grief care is important because one must ensure that the way they are processing grief is a healthy way to grieve.

We all grieve differently. Some find that writing and expressing their thoughts are helpful at times. Whatever your therapy is, figure it out. Seek God to help you to get through. Loss can be difficult, but there are methods of coping. Some people enjoy talking to a therapist, counselor, or unbiased friend. This is not to be underestimated or eliminated. Some people enjoy yoga or meditation. Whatever it takes to cope, do it. You have to excel. Your loved ones would expect nothing but excellence from you. Take a moment to write down how you are making the best of every loss and how you cope and heal daily. You are loved!

Blessing 11: Grief Care

My Reflections

_____

_____

_____

_____

_____

_____

_____

_____

_____

_____

_____

_____

My Blessings

_____

_____

_____

_____

_____

_____

_____

_____

_____

_____

_____

_____

_____

Blessing 12: Listen

Behold, I stand at the door, and knock: if any man hear my voice, and open the door, I will come in to him, and will sup with him, and he with me. (Revelations 3:20)

Most of the time, everyone is so busy that adhering to hear what God is trying to say is impossible. He is saying to you, "Listen, My child." Listening takes being attentive, meaning that whatever distractions or situations that have you occupied have to be paused. God is always speaking, but we are not always listening.

And oh! If we just take the time to listen, we will be surprised at what God has been saying all along. Some may wonder how to put this into action to hear clearly what God is saying. All one would need to do is take time to get in a quiet place, meditate and pray. When we ask God for something, He will surely deliver. He will give you the desires of your heart. Spend consistent time with Him. He looks forward to our consistency.

Making these sacrifices will allow you to erase the outside noise and hear the voice of God. He may speak to you through bringing a situation to your remembrance or even through a thought. Actually, you will be surprised how God speaks. Take time to acknowledge that He knows the plan (Jeremiah 29:11). Therefore, why wouldn't we seek the One that holds our future? Take a moment and pay attention to what God is speaking to you. Jot those things down. How will you remain consistent with your attentiveness? You are attentive!

Blessing 12: Listen

My Reflections

_____

_____

_____

_____

_____

_____

_____

_____

_____

_____

_____

_____

My Blessings

_____

_____

_____

_____

_____

_____

_____

_____

_____

_____

_____

_____

_____

_____

Blessing 13: A Great Person

And I will make of you a great nation, and I will bless you and make your name great, so that you will be a blessing. (Genesis 12:2)

There is so much to say to you, Great Person. First and foremost, "You are so special." Please know that you are well on your way. Do not ever let anyone tell you that you cannot do something. Believe in yourself, Great Person! You must stand up to the naysayers, lift your head up high and do what you have been called to do. You can make it no matter what the odds are.

Your future's so bright, Great Person! If no one ever told you that you are beautiful, remember that you are. You are Beautiful! Rise above the odds and believe in yourself!

Reflect on ways that define you as a great person. Write down those things and what you will work on to continue thriving. You are great!

Blessing 13: A Great Person

My Reflections

My Blessings

_____

_____

_____

_____

_____

_____

_____

_____

_____

_____

_____

_____

_____

_____

_____

Blessing 14: Keep Evolving

And though your beginning was small,
your latter days will be very great.
(Job 8:7)

J ust in case you have forgotten, you've got it going on. You are evolving and not letting anyone tell you that you aren't sharp because of your past! You have been through so much, and you are just at a point where you know your worth. Many people look at you under-eyed with bitterness and unforgiveness. What people fail to realize is that you are past that stage.

You are diligently stepping into the realm that God has in store for you. Yet, people look at you, and they really don't understand how you keep moving forward. They are expecting you to break down. Well, let them keep looking, wondering, and spectating. While they are concerned about your business, you've opened businesses and hired staff. You've written books, started agencies, lost weight, canceled your debts, and continue to prosper in every area of your life! Keep evolving!

Make a list of ways to recognize that you have evolved. Then, reflect on those things and keep pushing forward. You are destined for greatness!

Blessing 14: Keep Evolving

My Reflections

_____

_____

_____

_____

_____

_____

_____

_____

_____

_____

_____

_____

My Blessings

_____

_____

_____

_____

_____

_____

_____

_____

_____

_____

_____

_____

_____

_____

Blessing 15: Just Wait!

Wait on the LORD: Be of good courage, and he shall strengthen thine heart: wait, I say, on the LORD.
(Psalm 27:14)

Waiting can be quite challenging at times. Just think about all that it entails. Waiting seems like an eternity. In the process of waiting, patience is surely developed. Sometimes it seems like what you are waiting for will never happen. As you wait, just try not to dwell on what you are waiting for or over-analyze the process.

And guess what? To your surprise, the wait will eventually be over, and what you aspired to do or receive will take place. Trust and believe it will happen. You are blessed beyond measure. Sometimes waiting is necessary. It's just like going to your car and cranking it up. You do not arrive to your destination the moment that you sit in the car. It takes some time to get where you are going. Life is the same way. Sometimes there are hiccups, speed-bumps, or even delays along the way. But guess what? You will still arrive. It's going to happen. Just WAIT!

Make a list of things you waited patiently for and how waiting was well worth it. Then, reflect and remember that just as those situations eventually worked out, everything else will. You are a gift!

Blessing 15: Just Wait!

My Reflections

_____

_____

_____

_____

_____

_____

_____

_____

_____

_____

_____

_____

My Blessings

_____

_____

_____

_____

_____

_____

_____

_____

_____

_____

_____

_____

_____

_____

_____

Blessing 16: Togetherness

Two are better than one; because they have a good
reward for their labour. (Ecclesiastes 4:9)

There is a great reward when you can collaborate well with others. Sharing ideas and life lessons with others can be such a blessing. Today's world consists of minds that are not being stimulated but dissimulated by the corruptible voices of negative influence. Wouldn't it be grand if leaders of influence truly influenced and encouraged in a positive way?

We need to continue to assist other sisters and brothers on their journey to being the best version of themselves. Togetherness takes putting pride and fear to the side, and it requires being humble and resilient. What if every person on earth lived by this motto? Can you imagine how grand this world would be? Instead of opposition, people would position one another in a place to grow and live their true best life on earth. Ask yourself if you are truly living by the motto of learning collectively. If not, try to humble yourself and work on learning from others.

Do you have a mentor? Are you genuinely willing to learn from others? Write down one person that is an inspiration to you. Make sure this person is excelling in an area you want to grow in. Then, decide how you will learn from that person to apply specific principles to your life. You will be surprised by the outcome. You are growing!

Blessing 16: Togetherness

My Reflections

_____

_____

_____

_____

_____

_____

_____

_____

_____

_____

_____

_____

My Blessings

Blessing 17: It's Happening!

And we know that in all things God works for the good of those who love him, who have been called according to his purpose. (Romans 8:28)

Can you believe it? It's happening! You are walking on purpose and fulfilling your dreams! It's been a long time coming for you! The world celebrates you for taking this leap of faith to do what you were created to do! Don't let the naysayers discourage you. Don't let the yes-sayers put too much pressure on you either. Everyone will have their own opinion and logic on how you should carry out God's plan, but stay focused on what you know in your heart to be true!

Reflect on your blessing and how this journey called life has blessed you abundantly. Congratulations! Your best is yet to come!

Blessing 17: It's Happening!

My Reflections

_____

_____

_____

_____

_____

_____

_____

_____

_____

_____

_____

_____

My Blessings

Blessing 18: You are One

*But seek first the kingdom of God and his righteousness,
and all these things will be added to you.
(Matthew 6:33)*

You are one! Yes, you are one. One is singular and not plural. Continue to remind yourself that you are one. As you age, one begins to feel like a half. It sometimes seems like the things you once accomplished in a timely manner now take a little extra time.

On the flip side, with age comes wisdom, and with wisdom comes so much more. The additional demands of life can be overbearing. What you must tell yourself is, "You are one." Keeping this in mind, you can get the things done that are necessary when you prioritize first.

Strategize a plan and effectively complete the tasks presented to you. You are the one who can complete all of the tasks ahead of you. You are not half of one; you are a whole one. Plan, balance, and take the initiative to complete what you desire to do! You are the One! Make notes of how you will balance today and its tasks. Become in alignment with God! You can do it!

Blessing 18: You are One

My Reflections

_____

_____

_____

_____

_____

_____

_____

_____

_____

_____

_____

_____

_____

My Blessings

Blessing 19: The Dusty Road

*Show me the right path, O Lord; point out the road for
me to follow. (Psalm 25:4)*

The road is a little dusty, but you should keep driving. You'll have to pump your brakes from time to time. The road is a little curvy now, but you should keep going. Just keep your destination in mind. You may have to decrease speed just a little, but keep going. The road seems to have so many bumpy spots, but keep going and stay on course. You may have to proceed with caution, but keep going.

The road less traveled is the dusty, curvy, and bumpy one. Most people would instead take the main road, but this road is the road that God has destined for you. You are not the typical person, and you surely don't have a typical purpose or destination. Keep traveling the road less traveled, and you will see why

God had this road explicitly designed for you. You will be thankful that you kept driving. Keep going!

Reflect on areas of your life that are a little dusty. Acknowledge how you will keep going and never give up. You will reach your destination!

Blessing 19: The Dusty Road

My Reflections

_____

_____

_____

_____

_____

_____

_____

_____

_____

_____

_____

_____

_____

My Blessings

Blessing 20: Self-Check

And he said unto me, My grace is sufficient for thee: for
my strength is made perfect in weakness.
(2 Corinthians 12:9)

In this life, people say that only the strong survive. Okay, well, the strong get weak too and need to be checked on from time to time. Everyone has faced many challenges, and strong people are often a forgotten population of people. Many people see you and congratulate you for being able to overcome everything. Little do they realize, life is real for you too. Make sure that you check in with yourself and ensure that you are doing fine. Being persistent about a self-check is a great idea.

As you reflect today, ask yourself, "Are you truly okay?" Whatever your response is, it is the perfect opportunity to reach out to a friend or your support system. Be honest with yourself and if you are fine, share how great you are doing with someone. If you are not feeling at your best, share with someone you confide in. It is better to be supported than suffer in silence. You will win!

Blessing 20: Self-Check

My Reflections

_____

_____

_____

_____

_____

_____

_____

_____

_____

_____

_____

_____

My Blessings

_____

_____

_____

_____

_____

_____

_____

_____

_____

_____

_____

_____

_____

_____

Blessing 21: Note to Self

Jesus said to him, "If you can believe, all things are possible to him who believes." (Mark 9:23)

What are some things that you have resonated with so far? What are those friendly reminders that you need to tell yourself? Take a moment and jot down those things about yourself that maybe you had forgotten about.

Reminding yourself who you are will help you face difficulties and show up with confidence and boldness for any occasion. You are always winning!

Blessing 21: Note to Self

My Reflections

_____

_____

_____

_____

_____

_____

_____

_____

_____

_____

_____

_____

My Blessings

_____

_____

_____

_____

_____

_____

_____

_____

_____

_____

_____

_____

_____

_____

_____

Blessing 22: Revolving Relationships

*Iron sharpeneth iron; so a man sharpeneth the
countenance of his friend. (Proverbs 27:17)*

P
lease understand that people enter and exit
our lives all the time. You may start a job and
bond so well with your coworkers, and then
what do you know, they relocate. You may build a
new friendship or relationship thinking that it will
grow and become something great. It may or may not.
Sometimes relationships and friendships are only
temporary. If they are meant to last, they will last.
Some people feel down when friendships end
prematurely in their eyes. You cannot make people
remain in your life. Why have a pity party over who
exited when you can celebrate with the people who
remained?

So at this moment, lift your head and let those
relationships go! Move on with your life and water
seeds that are meant to grow in your life. Reflect on

those individuals that are dear to you. Be intentional about letting them know how appreciative you are. Make a list of those people and how they add to your life. You are cared about!

Blessing 22: Revolving Relationships

My Reflections

_____

_____

_____

_____

_____

_____

_____

_____

_____

_____

_____

_____

_____

My Blessings

_____

_____

_____

_____

_____

_____

_____

_____

_____

_____

_____

_____

_____

_____

_____

Blessing 23: Radiant You

*Let your light so shine before men, that they may see
your good works, and glorify your Father
which is in heaven. (Matthew 5:16)*

You are radiant. When you let your light shine, you are walking in your purpose. You are empowering the woman or man you were called to be. In doing so, you have decided to defy the odds. You are not allowing society or the media to impact your walk. You are allowing your God-given glow to protrude past who people say you should be. You are radiant! You are letting your shine follow you everywhere you go.

Let your light shine and be the best version of yourself! Reflect on ways that you will continue to let your radiant light shine. You are radiant!

Blessing 23: Radiant You

My Reflections

_____

_____

_____

_____

_____

_____

_____

_____

_____

_____

_____

_____

My Blessings

_____

_____

_____

_____

_____

_____

_____

_____

_____

_____

_____

_____

_____

_____

_____

_____

Blessing 24: Breathe!

Fear not, for I am with you; be not dismayed, for I am your God; I will strengthen you, I will help you, I will uphold you with my righteous right hand. (Isaiah 41:10)

Have you ever allowed your emotions to get the best of you? Have you ever reacted or responded impulsively? It's nothing to be ashamed of. It happens. Sometimes things occur unexpectedly, and reactions happen. Most of the time, the matters that bring significant distress change when your perspective changes.

Take a moment and breathe. All things are working for your good (Romans 8:28). Pause and take a deep breath; inhale and exhale. Now, write down those things that you need to gain perspective on.

Pray and allow God to show you those situations and people how He sees them. Then, be obedient and move forward in a manner that helps you to maintain your peace and a healthy mind. You are a breath of fresh air!

Blessing 24: Breathe!

My Reflections

_____

_____

_____

_____

_____

_____

_____

_____

_____

_____

_____

_____

_____

My Blessings

_____

_____

_____

_____

_____

_____

_____

_____

_____

_____

_____

_____

_____

_____

_____

_____

Blessing 25: Stand and Deliver!

I am strong and courageous. I will not be afraid of anyone, for the Lord my God goes with me. He will not fail me or forsake me. (Deuteronomy 31:6)

Wow! When others see you, they see a ray of sunshine. You don't even realize how your demeanor and posture reflect in the human eye. It's a vibe that is unexplainable. You are one of a kind. When you walk into a room, everyone feels a sense of warmth, and they are instantly energized by your glow. Because you bring so much to the table, you are irreplaceable.

Your shine comes from God, and you are expected to deliver. Your daily faith walk is obvious. Continue to be the remarkable being that you were created to be.

What are you saying to yourself these days? Jot those things down. However, positive vibes are only allowed. Remember, you are the vibe!

Blessing 25: Stand and Deliver!

My Reflections

_____

_____

_____

_____

_____

_____

_____

_____

_____

_____

_____

_____

My Blessings

_____

_____

_____

_____

_____

_____

_____

_____

_____

_____

_____

_____

_____

_____

_____

Blessing 26: Compadre

He that walketh with wise men shall be wise: but a companion of fools shall be destroyed. (Proverbs 13:20)

Compadres develop close connections, bonds, support, growth experiences, and aligned purpose. You may have met so many people from all walks of life. Be thankful for those individuals. Even if some were good and some not so good, those experiences were for your growth. Your close friendships were destined to be a part of the journey and probably have been for a while.

All of you may be in different places in your lives; however, you can add to one another's growth and genuinely have each other's best interests at heart. You should have a close connection, which is divine. The bonds of a compadre are not envious, jealous, or hateful. True friendships are ordained by God.

Now the hard part... Evaluate your circle. Do you have people in your circle that you need to distance yourself from? Ask yourself that question. Sometimes, your progress is stagnant because of the people you are connected to. Take a moment and evaluate your circle. Be clear that you are surrounded by authenticity. You are a great compadre!

Blessing 26: Compadre

My Reflections

_____

_____

_____

_____

_____

_____

_____

_____

_____

_____

_____

_____

_____

My Blessings

_____

_____

_____

_____

_____

_____

_____

_____

_____

_____

_____

_____

_____

_____

Blessing 27: You Think You Know, But You Have No Idea

"For my thoughts are not your thoughts,
neither are your ways my ways," declares the Lord.
"As the heavens are higher than the earth, so are my
ways higher than your ways and my thoughts than
your thoughts." (Isaiah 55:8-9)

S ome situations arise, and you think you have it all figured out, but you really have no idea. You may analyze and be able to look at the glass half full and not half empty. Therefore, knowing that you will not always be right about *everything*, sometimes you just have to take a step back and breathe. Just know that it's okay to not know, and it's okay to feel how you feel about it. As long as your thoughts and feelings don't fester and consume you.

In the midst of uncertainty, keep in mind that whatever the outcome is, all is well. All *will be* well. Things always work out the way that they are supposed to. Some situations are beyond your control; therefore, you must accept what God allows and move on. Life teaches you to embrace every moment and know that the outcome will shape, mold, and make you.

With this being said, walk out your destiny and purpose knowing that *All is Well* and you've got this! What are some things that you are sorting through? Jot those things down and be okay with not understanding the outcome. Be prayerful and even talk about the situation with someone you confide in. You are purposeful!

Blessing 27: You Think You Know, But You Have No Idea

My Reflections

_____

_____

_____

_____

_____

_____

_____

_____

_____

_____

_____

My Blessings

Blessing 28: It Will Work Out!

For I know the thoughts that I think toward you, saith the LORD, thoughts of peace, and not of evil, to give you an expected end. (Jeremiah 29:11)

Your situation will work out. It will work out in a way that you would not believe. Yes, it hurts now, but you are healing. It's not a good feeling, but you will come out on top. Focus on Jeremiah 29:11. God has plans to prosper you and not to harm you. As you continue to study this Scripture, you will find that He plans to give you hope and a future.

With that being said, rest in His arms, knowing that every area of your life is covered by Him. God is going to bless you real good. Stay focused and know that your blessings are near and everything will work out. Write down those situations, cross them out, and write on top of them, *Jeremiah 29:11*. You are prosperous!

Blessing 28: It Will Work Out!

My Reflections

_____

_____

_____

_____

_____

_____

_____

_____

_____

_____

_____

_____

My Blessings

_____

_____

_____

_____

_____

_____

_____

_____

_____

_____

_____

_____

_____

Blessing 29: Think About Your Life

Commit thy works unto the Lord, and thy thoughts shall be established. (Proverbs 16:3)

As you think about your life and as you think about your existence, what do you realize? Pause from reading this for a quick second and reflect on your life. Are you where you want to be? Have you allowed yourself to be limited in your thinking? Have you conquered and accomplished those things you know God has spoken to you? Think about how you are reminded of how God wants to use you.

Today is your day to get started. Today is your day to think about your life in a new way. Make the best of every situation. It is your time to thrive in your thinking and allow God to order your steps and guide you. As you think about your life, see yourself happy, living accomplished, and walking out everything God has spoken to you. See yourself taking every step you thought you would not have taken. Then, write down what you have discovered today. What measure will you take to walk in alignment with your purpose? You are in alignment!

Blessing 29: Think About Your Life

My Reflections

_____

_____

_____

_____

_____

_____

_____

_____

_____

_____

_____

_____

My Blessings

_____

_____

_____

_____

_____

_____

_____

_____

_____

_____

_____

_____

_____

_____

_____

_____

Blessing 30: Another Day, Another Blessing

Blessed be the Lord, who daily loadeth us with benefits, even the God of our salvation. Selah. (Psalm 68:19)

Y ou've been blessed to see another day. Be thankful for this day. Look back and see all of the ways that you've been blessed through every situation. Daily, the Lord loads you with His benefits, which are out of this world.

Remain humble and grateful. Reflect on your life lessons and acknowledge your strength. You are strong!

Blessing 30: Another Day, Another Blessing

My Reflections

_____

_____

_____

_____

_____

_____

_____

_____

_____

_____

_____

_____

My Blessings

Blessing 31: To-Do List

*Set your affection on things above,
not on things on the earth. (Colossians 3:2)*

There are always things to do. Determine what is important and do just that! Prioritize and keep your focus. You will accomplish exactly what you want to do.

Write down your priorities for today. Be mindful and intentional about your priorities. You are prioritizing!

Blessing 31: To-Do List

My Reflections

_____

_____

_____

_____

_____

_____

_____

_____

_____

_____

_____

_____

_____

My Blessings

Blessing 32: Kind Hearts

And be ye kind one to another, tenderhearted, forgiving one another, even as God for Christ's sake hath forgiven you. (Ephesians 4:32)

Do you have a kind heart? The answer is yes or no. It should not take time to think about the answer to this question. So do you have a kind heart?

When we think of the word *kind*, we think of something or someone pleasant. But your heart says so much about you. Some people strive to have a kind heart; however, the heart is shattered due to their past experiences. This makes it unpleasant. What do you do when you can't erase the past? Nor how it has affected your heart and its ability to give your all to someone or to something. It may take time but work towards developing the strength to understand your heart and its capabilities to be kind. Sometimes just a deep glance into what is causing your unhealthy heart will prepare you for greater friendships, relationships, and self-love. Write down how you will examine your heart and work towards healing. You are kind-hearted!

Blessing 32: Kind Hearts

My Reflections

_____

_____

_____

_____

_____

_____

_____

_____

_____

_____

_____

_____

_____

My Blessings

_____

_____

_____

_____

_____

_____

_____

_____

_____

_____

_____

_____

_____

_____

Blessing 33: Encourage Others

Therefore encourage one another and build one another up, just as you are doing. (1 Thessalonians 5:11)

C heck in on your loved ones. They need love too. Sometimes people suffer in silence, and you'd be surprised how your voice could mend a broken heart.

Reflect on times that you have made someone's day. Have you spoken positively or encouraged anyone lately? Be intentional about listing three people you care about. Then, plan to check on them today. A quick phone call will add joy to their soul as well as yours. You are an encourager!

Blessing 33: Encourage Others

My Reflections

_____

_____

_____

_____

_____

_____

_____

_____

_____

_____

_____

_____

My Blessings

_____

_____

_____

_____

_____

_____

_____

_____

_____

_____

_____

_____

_____

_____

Blessing 34: You are Special

But ye are a chosen generation, a royal priesthood, an holy nation, a peculiar people; that ye should shew forth the praises of him who hath called you out of darkness into his marvellous light: (1 Peter 2:9)

Let no one tell you that you are not special because you are. You are just who you are supposed to be, which is extraordinary. Just remember that you hold the key to your future. All you have to do is believe and try. Don't let how you feel now change how you feel about your incredible life.

Your life is special, and you are too. Go after your dreams so that the world will witness how special you are. Don't let everyone miss out on the extraordinary you. Every day strive to be the best you. You are unique in your own way. Be you, and let no one take your place. They couldn't do it anyway because you are uniquely designed. Write down those things that make you unique. Then, celebrate those things by treating yourself to something special today. You are one of a kind!

Blessing 34: You are Special

My Reflections

_____

_____

_____

_____

_____

_____

_____

_____

_____

_____

_____

_____

My Blessings

_____

_____

_____

_____

_____

_____

_____

_____

_____

_____

_____

_____

_____

Blessing 35: Your Opinion

Death and life are in the power of the tongue.
(Proverbs 18:21)

An opinion is what you think or feel about someone or something. Some people really mistake their opinion for facts. Facts, however, are true, and you can prove them. Some people place input in areas that they lack knowledge of. Some people have their opinions about things that are irrelevant. *If it's not factual, it's not actual.*

Remember to speak on what you know. Avoid unnecessary lingo that does not positively benefit you or the person you discuss matters with. Being mindful of the tongue and what comes out of the mouth is a strategy used toward success and being purposeful.

What are you discussing these days? Are your words adding life or terminating life? Reflect on the words that you speak daily. Evaluate the context of the last conversation that you had. Was it uplifting? You are

a person of integrity!

Blessing 35: Your Opinion

My Reflections

_____

_____

_____

_____

_____

_____

_____

_____

_____

_____

_____

_____

My Blessings

Blessing 36: Tomorrow

Therefore do not worry about tomorrow, for tomorrow will worry about itself. Each day has enough trouble of its own. (Matthew 6:34)

As the door closes, the last words you hear are, "I'll see you tomorrow." At that very moment, it seems like tomorrow will be millions of years away. What do you do within the very hour of them leaving? Tears are shed in hopes they'll be back to ask if you need a tissue. You try to escape the very fact that they are no longer there.

Anything can happen between now and tomorrow is what your heart and mind say. Tomorrow must be a long word because it seems so far away, especially when the one you love and care for leaves your presence. As the minutes trickle by, feelings of detachment, separation, disconnect, and withdrawal are what you continue to experience. You start to think, how can I transform tomorrow into today? Then suddenly, you wake up and realize that it was just a dream! Your tomorrow is really today, and your love never left. It was all a dream; tomorrow is today!

What dream are you waking up from? What are you just now realizing is really a blessing? What or who are you worried about instead of giving the matter to God? Write those things down and then turn them over to God. You are unbothered!

Blessing 36: Tomorrow

My Reflections

_____

_____

_____

_____

_____

_____

_____

_____

_____

_____

_____

_____

My Blessings

_____

_____

_____

_____

_____

_____

_____

_____

_____

_____

_____

_____

_____

_____

Blessing 37: The Journey Begins

Consider it pure joy, my brothers and sisters, whenever you face trials of many kinds because you know that the testing of your faith produces perseverance. Let perseverance finish its work so that you may be mature and complete, not lacking anything. (James 1:2-4)

Yes indeed, the journey begins! But, it is not as long as you think that it is. Nor is it as daring as you thought. Especially if you allow God to guide you. Surely, it will be filled with adventure and life learning experiences. However, try not to go through the same tests over and over. Learn from those things that you go through on the journey. Pray along the way without ceasing. The Lord has you, and you will be thankful for the journey and appreciative that it began.

Write down some of your life lessons. What have you learned about yourself through this journey called life? Note what tests have strengthened your faith. You are graced for the journey!

Blessing 37: The Journey Begins

My Reflections

_____

_____

_____

_____

_____

_____

_____

_____

_____

_____

_____

_____

My Blessings

Blessing 38: The Curveball

Be strong and of good courage, do not fear nor be afraid of them; for the Lord your God, He is the One who goes with you. He will not leave you nor forsake you.
(Deuteronomy 31:6)

L ife will surely throw you some curveballs. Each time you learn to duck quicker and faster. You will be thankful that you went through those experiences and the curves. Every now and then, a detour may be necessary, and that may be highlighted through life's curveballs.

Instead of complaining, appreciate the ability to step your game up and face whatever comes your way. Now, reflect on a detour that you had to make. What did you learn? You are stronger than you will ever know!

Blessing 38: The Curveball

My Reflections

_____

_____

_____

_____

_____

_____

_____

_____

_____

_____

_____

_____

My Blessings

_____

_____

_____

_____

_____

_____

_____

_____

_____

_____

_____

_____

_____

_____

Blessing 39: Testimonies

*I will speak of thy testimonies also before kings
and will not be ashamed. (Psalm 119:46)*

I f you shared all of your testimonies with someone, they would be amazed! Life has genuinely shown you God's love, yourself, and others. Everything that has happened really was a way to shift your thinking and readjust your life to focus on God.

When you look at yourself, you should see the beauty of going through to get to all God had and still has in store for you! You had to go through to get through! Reflect on your testimonies! Write them down and share them with someone going through tests and trials. You went through to help someone along the way! You are brilliant!

Blessing 39: Testimonies

My Reflections

_____

_____

_____

_____

_____

_____

_____

_____

_____

_____

_____

_____

_____

My Blessings

Blessing 40: Creating a New U

Therefore, if anyone is in Christ, the new creation has come: The old has gone, the new is here!
(2 Corinthians 5:17)

My my my! Look at you! You have really shown up and shown out. You are the true definition of a game-changer! You are walking in your purpose! Every time your name rolls off someone's tongue, they say that you are blessed and that your blessings continue to chase you down! Look at all the favor and flavor upon your life. Everyone is proud of you. You are representing and showing up as the ultimate version of yourself. So, reflect and celebrate a new you! God's Grace Created A New U!

Blessing 40: Creating a New U

My Reflections

_____

_____

_____

_____

_____

_____

_____

_____

_____

_____

_____

_____

_____

My Blessings

Blessing 41: Creating A New U Affirmations

- ♥ *I'm fabulous, free, and focused!*

- ♥ *I'm grateful, grand, and glowing!*

- ♥ *I'm awesome, amazing, and authentic!*

- ♥ *I'm beautiful, bold, and breaking barriers!*

- ♥ *I'm a winning worshipping warrior!*

- ♥ *I'm praying, passionate, and purpose-filled!*

- ♥ *I'm God's Glowing Girl/Guy!*

- ♥ *I'm daring, decisive, and dedicated!*

- ♥ *I'm a caring, compassionate conqueror!*

- ♥ *I'm healed, healthy, and heard!*

- ♥ *I'm laughing, loving, and listening!*

- ♥ *I'm accomplishing, acknowledging, and awaiting!*

♥ *I'm decreeing, declaring, and dancing!*

♥ *I'm forgiving, faithful, and fearless!*

♥ *I'm representing, reaping, and real!*

♥ *I'm sowing, serving, and shining!*

♥ *I'm celebrating, creating, and consistent!*

♥ *I'm leading, loving, and learning!*

♥ *I am wise, winning, and walking in wholeness!*

Additional Reflections & Blessings Pages

My Reflections

_____

_____

_____

_____

_____

_____

_____

_____

_____

_____

_____

_____

_____

My Blessings

_____

_____

_____

_____

_____

_____

_____

_____

_____

_____

_____

_____

My Reflections

My Blessings

My Reflections

_____

_____

_____

_____

_____

_____

_____

_____

_____

_____

_____

_____

My Blessings

My Reflections

My Blessings

_____

_____

_____

_____

_____

_____

_____

_____

_____

_____

_____

_____

_____

_____

_____

My Reflections

My Blessings

_____

_____

_____

_____

_____

_____

_____

_____

_____

_____

_____

_____

_____

MEET THE AUTHOR

Richonda Hill began creating this reflection journal through an online blog in 2018. She calls it, "From Blogs to Blessings." She has always enjoyed journaling and blogging, as writing became one of her fulfilling hobbies at a very young age. Richonda has always been a woman who loves to inspire others and counts this as a blessing to impact the lives of others. She also takes time to reread and reflect on her blog/journal entries and gains inspiration from her very own words.

Richonda believes that everyone could use an extra nudge as they journey through life. She believes that "41 Blessings" will be the best friend you can't reach when you are going through. It will be the close relative that told you they will call you right back when you really need some advice immediately. She wrote "41 Blessings" just for YOU as a tour guide through life. She believes that there is so much power in being selective about what you read. From the youngest person to the oldest person, "41 Blessings" will give you the hope, confidence, and boldness that you need as you count your many blessings.

Made in the USA
Middletown, DE
10 May 2022

65571077R00096